BUILT FOR SUCCESS

THE STORY OF

FedEx

Published by Creative Education
P.O. Box 227, Mankato, Minnesota 56002
Creative Education is an imprint of The Creative Company
www.thecreativecompany.us

DESIGN BY **ZENO DESIGN**
PRODUCTION BY **CHRISTINE VANDERBEEK**
ART DIRECTION BY **RITA MARSHALL**

Printed by Corporate Graphics in the United States of America

PHOTOGRAPHS BY Alamy (AF archive, NetPhotos), AP Images
(Associated Press), Corbis (GENE BLEVINS/Reuters, Reuters),
Getty Images (Daniel Acker, Jeremy Bales/Bloomberg, Nelson
Ching/Bloomberg, Andrew Harrer/Bloomberg, Chris Hondros,
Hisham Ibrahim, Peter Kramer, Scott Olson, PAUL J.
RICHARDS/AFP, STR/AFP, BOB STRONG/AFP, Justin Sullivan,
Greg Whitesell, iStockphoto (David Birkbeck), The Commercial
Appeal (James R. Reid)

LIBRARY OF CONGRESS CATALOGING-IN-PUBLICATION DATA

Gilbert, Sara.
The story of FedEx / by Sara Gilbert.
p. cm. — (Built for success)
Summary: A look at the origins, leaders, growth, and innova-
tions of FedEx, a logistics corporation that was founded in
1971 and today is one of the largest international shipping
companies in the world.
Includes bibliographical references and index.
ISBN 978-1-60818-177-3
1. FedEx Corporation—Juvenile literature. 2. Freight and
freightage—United States—Juvenile literature. 3. Aeronautics,
Commercial—Freight—Juvenile literature. I. Title. II. Series.

HE199.U5G55 2012
388'.0440973—dc23   2011035755

First edition

9 8 7 6 5 4 3 2 1

THE STORY OF

FedEx

Express

SARA GILBERT

As the sun set on April 17, 1973, a parade of airplanes began to touch down at the headquarters of Federal Express in Memphis, Tennessee. The 14 planes were greeted by many of the company's almost 400 employees, including founder Fred Smith. As soon as the planes came to a stop, the employees unloaded and processed the 186 packages that had been collected from 25 cities across the country that day—the first packages ever handled by the company. Before the sun came up, all of the packages were loaded back onto the airplanes, ready to be delivered to their intended recipients the next day. Smith was tired at daybreak, but he was ready to do it again the next night—and his company would keep doing it for more than 40 years to come.

CHAPTER ONE

Getting off the Ground

In the mid-1960s, when Fred Smith was a sophomore **economics** major at Yale University, he wrote a paper for a class describing an overnight **courier** service that was built around a "hub-and-spoke" concept of collecting and delivering packages in America.

He envisioned a fleet of airplanes picking up packages, bringing them to a central "hub" location, and then branching out like spokes to rapidly deliver them all over the country. Smith's professor wasn't impressed by the premise, but the idea lingered in Smith's mind.

After graduating in 1966 and serving in the Marines during the Vietnam War, Smith took control of his stepfather's Little Rock, Arkansas-based business, which sold fuel to pilots of small planes and rented out **hangar** space. Smith started repairing corporate jets and developed a reputation for quick response times and low costs. But he was frustrated by delays in the shipping of necessary parts; a "rush" delivery might take seven days.

That frustration was on Smith's mind when he decided to start a new business. He wanted to develop a flight courier service to transport time-sensitive checks and financial documents between the Federal Reserve, the central banking system in the United States, and the banks that it oversaw. The Federal

Fred Smith personally directed the growth of FedEx throughout its first four decades of existence.

Reserve Board appeared interested in the idea when Smith met with them in 1971, so he started building the business. With money inherited from his late father, additional funds from investors, and a $3.6-million loan, Smith bought and modified two French-built Dassault Falcon jets, and in June, he **incorporated** his new business as Federal Express. But then the Federal Reserve backed out of the deal, declaring the proposed change too disruptive to established banking schedules.

Smith was disappointed but not discouraged. He changed his focus to overnight package delivery, a service that was being offered in only a few major cities at the time. Smith believed that he could make the service more widely available around the country. He recruited a small, high-level management team that was instrumental not only in developing the business plan and designing the operations but also in finding funding for Federal Express. Unfortunately, many investors were skittish about the risks associated with the business. Although Smith and his team were able to pull together enough money and secure enough loans to cover startup costs, they weren't able to obtain a large investment that would ensure the company's long-term growth.

Smith was undeterred. He hired a corps of delivery drivers, known as couriers, who would present a professional, polite appearance when making pickups or deliveries at an office building. Smith personally called people to ask them to join his company as sales agents, customer service staff, and couriers, promising that they would be trained well and paid fairly and that, eventually, they would have the opportunity to share in the company's **profits**. Before the company officially started operations, Smith emphasized that its culture would put people first, service second, and profits third.

In January 1973, Smith relocated the business from Little Rock to the airport in Memphis, Tennessee, intending to begin service on March 12. When the sales team managed to collect only six packages that day, they decided to call those first deliveries a successful "system test" and to officially start operations in

The Federal Reserve, America's central banking system, was formed in 1913 and headquartered in Washington, D.C.

April. "We are going to do it right this time," Smith told the company's 389 employees. "Failure is not an option." This time, almost 200 packages were picked up by Federal Express couriers, flown to Memphis, and then shipped to 25 U.S. cities, including Chicago, Detroit, New Orleans, and Cleveland.

By the end of June, Federal Express was shipping more than 1,000 packages daily to almost 35 cities, having expanded its service to cover Boston, Wichita, Baltimore, and other locations. But the company's finances were so unstable that one pilot used his personal credit card to cover the landing fees at an airport, and a courier sold his watch to help pay for fuel for the van. At one point, when only $5,000 remained in the corporate account on a Friday evening and a $24,000 fuel bill was due the following Monday, Smith took the last of the money to Las Vegas, where he tried to win more by gambling. On Monday morning, there was almost $32,000 in the account.

Despite Smith's lucky winnings, the company was dangerously behind on its bills and on the brink of **bankruptcy**. Relief arrived on November 13, 1973, when a **venture capital** group invested $24.5 million in Federal Express and guaranteed long-term loans for another $27.5 million. With cash in hand, Smith signed bonus checks for all of his employees.

But then oil-producing nations such as Saudi Arabia, Iran, and Iraq decided to place an **embargo** on oil, causing a fuel shortage all over the world. In the U.S., fuel prices soared. Federal Express had to negotiate an **allocation** of fuel with the government and find a supplier able to provide more than 4 million gallons (15 million l) for the next year's flights. With fuel flowing from Exxon, Federal Express shipped more than 100,000 packages a month during the 1973 holiday season. By the middle of 1974, Federal Express was shipping more than 10,000 pieces a day—and most of them were arriving on time, thanks to Smith's insistence on superior customer service at every level.

> "At FedEx, our people and our culture distinguish us from the competition—and we are particularly proud of our unique focus on service and innovation."
>
> FRED SMITH, FEDEX FOUNDER

FedEx's success—from its start to today—has always depended upon swift and careful package sorting

Fred Smith, pictured in 1983

UP IN THE AIR

Fred Smith grew up in the air. He was so fascinated with airplanes and flight that, as a teenager, he became an amateur pilot. While at Yale University in the mid-1960s, he resurrected the Yale Flying Club—an organization that had first been started in the 1930s—and flew with John Kerry, who later became a U.S. senator from Massachusetts. Although he hired pilots and purchased airplanes as the chief executive officer (CEO) of FedEx, Smith was grounded most of the time after founding the company. For many years, he made time to maintain his pilot's license and keep his skills sharp, but by the late 1990s he was too busy to fit it in. "I really had to work hard to keep the flying up," he said in an interview in 2001. "I used to go out on the weekends and do acrobatics and that kind of stuff."

CHAPTER TWO

Flying High

Business continued to increase for FedEx, as the company became known, but the costs of building the business and maintaining its fleet of vehicles did, too. By the end of 1975, Federal Express had lost more than $29 million in its first 3 years of existence.

But during that time, the company had also built the **infrastructure** it needed to start making money. It was preparing to add to its original fleet of 14 planes. It had established drop-off and pickup facilities from which drivers were dispatched in nearly every major U.S. city. It had positioned itself as the premier overnight delivery service in operation, better than such competitors as United Parcel Service (UPS) and Emery Air Freight, partly because it didn't rely on commercial flights to ferry its packages from point to point. Its reputation for reliable overnight service was one of its greatest assets and one of the reasons it was able to report its first profit, of $3.6 million, in 1976.

What it needed next was a little help from the U.S. government. Federal laws regulating the capacity of cargo airlines limited the size of planes that FedEx could use, which was in turn limiting the company's capability to continue growing. Already, Federal Express's volume had grown so much that the company was forced to arrange for supplemental charter flights to help deliver its

The 1970s growth of FedEx was made possible in part by the increased size of its cargo planes

packages. In addition, some of its planes were making double trips in one night, and the company had even started trucking some packages to nearby locations. "It was clear that this was only a temporary solution," said Roger Frock, the general manager of FedEx at the time.

Smith had been **lobbying** Congress for two years when, on November 9, 1977, president Jimmy Carter granted FedEx and similar airline services the right to use the larger aircraft they needed without restrictions on routes. With that legal obstacle out of the way, FedEx purchased and modified 7 Boeing 727 jets that could each carry 40,000 pounds (18,144 kg) of cargo—almost 7 times what it had been able to load into the Falcon aircraft in its fleet.

Suddenly, Federal Express's future seemed more secure than ever, and the company's board agreed that it was time to make it a public company by selling **shares** on the **stock** market. The 783,000 shares that were sold on April 12, 1978, for $24 apiece raised $18.8 million. FedEx employees purchased 635,000 shares, which Smith had reserved for them at a slightly discounted rate in appreciation of the sacrifices many of them had made in the process of building the company.

With solid funding in place and business still growing, FedEx started making investments in its future by introducing technology-based advancements to streamline customer service. The initiatives, which were launched in 1979 from the company's new research and development center in Colorado Springs, Colorado, included a centralized computer system called COSMOS. (The **acronym** stood for Customers, Operations, and Services Master Online System.) COSMOS made it possible for customers to request a package pickup with a phone call to the centralized customer service center in Memphis and for that information to be passed directly to the relevant FedEx driver through small computers installed in the company's thousands of trucks. Such early technological advances allowed FedEx to both pick up and deliver packages more efficiently, giving it a distinct advantage over its competitors.

Like Fred Smith, Georgian Jimmy Carter—in office as president from 1977 to 1981—hailed from the South.

In the midst of the excitement over Federal Express's growth emerged a problem: the company's Memphis hub was struggling to handle the volume of packages coming through daily. Although there was talk of opening three additional hubs in strategic locations around the country, the company decided instead to upgrade the site in Memphis to become a "superhub." The new and improved facility opened next to the Memphis airport in 1981, shortly before FedEx initiated its first international service to Canada.

That same year, FedEx began a new service to the business community by offering the Overnight Letter—a document-sized envelope that could be shipped for the flat fee of $9.50 (other packages were priced according to weight). But Smith wanted to offer businesses an even faster, more convenient way to send documents, so he started developing ZapMail. The plan was to use high-quality fax machines to deliver electronic documents from one business to another in less than two hours. He was so committed to the concept that he devoted most of the company's resources to it, putting further international expansion and other ideas on the back burner to do so.

Smith spent 3 years and almost $100 million developing ZapMail before launching the service in 1984. Unfortunately, it was plagued with problems from the beginning, due in large part to the technology available for fax transmissions at the time. The machines broke down often, and when they worked, the quality of the faxed documents couldn't be guaranteed. The short-lived service was discontinued two years later.

In the meantime, however, the next-day delivery business that had been FedEx's core offering from the beginning was going gangbusters—despite new competition from the U.S. Postal Service, which had introduced its own overnight delivery service, and UPS, which had launched an air-express service in 1981. Business was so good, in fact, that in 1983, just 10 years after the company was founded, Federal Express reported $1 billion in annual **revenue**.

"FedEx clearly is not resting on its laurels of having invented a business. They are constantly expanding."

KEN HOEXTER, STOCK MARKET ANALYST

FedEx's Memphis hub became almost a small city, eventually employing more than 10,000 workers

When Federal Express officially shortened its name to FedEx in 1994, the company also updated its original purple, orange, and white "bubble letter" logo (for which company founder Fred Smith had paid $25,000 in 1972). The bold new logo, which was designed by graphic artist Lindon Leader, has since won more than 40 awards worldwide, including being ranked as one of the best logos since the mid-1970s by *Rolling Stone* magazine. Although it may look like nothing more than brightly colored block letters at first glance, an arrow was discreetly placed between the "E" and the "x," a representation of FedEx's speed and precision. Leader, who submitted almost 200 versions of the logo before it was approved, manipulated the fonts he used for the letters in the logo to create the space for the arrow, eventually blending them to achieve the right effect.

CHAPTER THREE

Going Global

Although FedEx had entered Canada, the company was still searching for the right way to cross both the Atlantic and Pacific oceans and expand its international reach. FedEx was especially interested in the Asian market, since more and more computer components and other products were being manufactured in Asia and shipped to the U.S. Federal Express wanted to play a major role in the shipping of those parts around the world.

It took its first step in that direction in 1984 with the **acquisition** of Gelco Express International, a Minneapolis-based courier company that operated in 84 countries in Europe and Asia. FedEx also acquired services in the United Kingdom, the Netherlands, and the United Arab Emirates—part of its strategy to purchase companies that already had landing rights at the international airports it would need to access. In 1985, it also opened a European hub at the Brussels, Belgium, airport.

FedEx's domestic operations were expanding as well. In 1986, the company built new sorting centers in Oakland, California, and Newark, New Jersey, to handle the enormous number of shipments headed to such popular nearby destinations as

Although China long resisted foreign businesses, FedEx persisted in its efforts to expand there.

Los Angeles and New York City. The company also began housing merchandise from some of its largest customers in its Memphis hub as well as its new sorting centers so that their products could be shipped on-demand directly from FedEx.

Once again, FedEx expanded its technological capabilities to improve customer service. In 1986, it introduced the SuperTracker, a handheld computer that couriers used to scan the bar code on every package at various stages of the delivery process, including pickup, final delivery, and three or four points in between. The information stored in each SuperTracker was loaded into the COSMOS system, which allowed customers to track their packages by simply calling customer service.

FedEx was doing quite well. Sales in 1985 hit $2 billion and doubled over the next four years. But while the company was still profitable, it faced growing competition from the U.S. Postal Service, which offered next-day delivery on certain packages for almost half the price FedEx charged. The increased competition led to a price war that prevented FedEx from implementing price increases, even as its expenses rose.

FedEx had to distinguish itself with something other than price, so the company made another strategic acquisition in 1989. For a cost of $895 million, it purchased the Flying Tigers, a cargo airline company with a fleet of more than 35 planes and established routes to 21 countries. Later that year, FedEx also opened a hub in Anchorage, Alaska. Both moves were questioned by experts; some thought the company had paid too much for the Flying Tigers, and many saw Anchorage as too remote to be an effective hub.

But both were part of FedEx's long-term plan to expand internationally and penetrate the Asian markets. Prior to the Flying Tigers purchase, FedEx had landing rights in only five international airports: Montreal and Toronto in Canada; Brussels, Belgium, and London, England, in Europe; and Tokyo in Japan, although its rights were limited there. Flying Tigers' existing relationships gave FedEx access to airports in Paris, France, and Frankfurt, Germany, as well as three

SAA 21690 F X

FedEx

PROPERTY
OF F

From letters to bulky cargo, FedEx set the industry standard for being able to track in-transit packages.

more Japanese airports and other sites throughout Asia and South America.

Anchorage also made sense on a number of levels. For one thing, the airport there was remarkably reliable—it rarely closed, even in the midst of snowstorms dropping 12 inches (30 cm) or more of snow. Plus, the city is just a 10-hour flight from almost 90 percent of the industrialized world. "A lot of people don't know this, but Anchorage is equidistant [the same distance] from London, New York, and Tokyo," Smith said. "So it's our top-of-the-world hub on a great circle route."

FedEx lost money on its international operations in 1989. The integration of the Flying Tigers into its system added costs, especially because many of the planes in the fleet needed significant repairs and upgrades. But FedEx was able to offset those losses slightly with growth in U.S. revenues, which were helped by the company's decision to end the price wars with its competitors and institute its first increase in domestic prices in seven years. The price change helped FedEx record revenues of $7 billion—a 36 percent increase over the previous year.

By 1990, Federal Express employed 94,000 people, from executives working in Memphis to pilots, drivers, customer service representatives, and sales agents around the world. Most of those employees agreed with Smith's insistence on 100 percent customer satisfaction ratings, and all of them were encouraged to be innovative in suggesting how to better serve customers. To keep customer service at the top of employees' minds, the company printed "A satisfied customer made this possible" on all paycheck envelopes.

In December 1990, FedEx was honored with the prestigious Malcolm Baldrige National Quality Award, which recognizes companies that not only provide quality customer service but also involve their employees in continually improving processes. As he accepted the award from U.S. president George H. W. Bush, Smith thanked his employees for their help. "From our beginning 17 years ago, nothing short of absolutely, positively 100 percent customer satisfaction has ever been acceptable," Smith said. "And we work to achieve it every day."

"FedEx has built what is the most seamless global air and ground network in its industry, connecting more than 90 percent of the world's economic activity."

WILLIAM G. MARGARITIS, FEDEX EXECUTIVE

A huge plane fleet and round-the-clock operations enable FedEx packages to cross the world in a day

HELPING HARRY

FedEx planes and trucks were especially busy on the morning of Saturday, July 8, 2000. That's the day that the company teamed up with online retailer Amazon.com to distribute 250,000 copies of *Harry Potter and the Goblet of Fire*, by J. K. Rowling, to eager young readers as soon as the book became available to the public. More than 9,000 FedEx delivery personnel used 100 FedEx flights and 700 company vehicles to execute the coordinated delivery of all 675,000 pounds (306,175 kg) of the books. "Not since Santa Claus, the elves, and the reindeer has one delivery made this many kids happy," an Amazon executive reported. Back at FedEx headquarters, the company's executive vice president of market development and corporate communications championed the success of the partnership. "This is a classic example of how the speed of online shopping can be combined with innovative fulfillment solutions to satisfy customers," T. Michael Glenn said.

CHAPTER FOUR

New Names, New Markets

By the early 1990s, Federal Express had gained a reputation around the world as the premier overnight delivery service. In many offices and homes, people even used the company's name as a verb, saying "FedEx it" when they wanted something shipped quickly.

That shortened version of its name had become so prevalent as both a verb and a noun, in fact, that in 1994, the company officially adopted it as the **brand** name for its package delivery business. Suddenly, the company's vast fleet of planes, vans, and trucks boasted six-foot-tall (1.8 m) dark purple and orange letters labeling the company as FedEx.

With its new name and striking logo in place, FedEx made another bold move, this time becoming the first courier service to build a site on the World Wide Web: www.fedex.com. The site, which launched in 1994, allowed customers to track the status of their packages. It eventually also enabled them to request a pickup online (instead of having to call customer service or drive the package to a drop-off point themselves).

Smith's primary intention was for FedEx to be the courier of choice all over the world, and he continued to work hard to make that happen. The company was

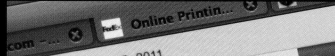

Tuesday, February 22, 2011

Copy & Print ▼ | Marketing Products

FedExOffice®

FedEx Kinko's is now FedEx Office

Welcome to FedEx Office

This is your destination for printing, document services and much more. Take advantage of products and features to meet your personal and business needs.

20

Get 20% off when you purc
Hurry, offer ends 3/6/11.

Get started ▸

FedEx Office® Print Onlin

Order Online

NEW DESIGN

Online

Web site developments in the 1990s helped make FedEx more customer-friendly than ever before

already the largest full-service cargo airline in the world and had established itself so strongly in Asia that by the summer of 1995 it was in the process of constructing a hub facility in the Philippines. But there was one country that FedEx still had not made any progress with at that point: China, which, with a population of more than one billion people, was a major player in the Asian economy. Then, in February 1995, FedEx purchased the Chinese cargo route authority from Evergreen International Airlines, an Oregon-based aviation company, and became the sole American cargo carrier able to do business in China. For FedEx, and for CEO Smith, that was a huge win. China, Smith said, was key to the company's long-term expansion plans because it represented the greatest growth potential. "Asia will be one of the great engines of growth in the next century," Smith said. "As the world's most populous country, China will be at the heart of much of that growth."

By 1996, at least 12 percent of FedEx's more than $10 billion in sales was generated by international operations. The company offered services in more than 200 countries and was easily outperforming its competitors internationally. Business was growing so well at home as well that the company opened another hub near Dallas, Texas, in 1997.

Then came the UPS **strike** in August 1997. For 15 days, FedEx's most serious competitor was completely shut down as its **union** employees walked out, refusing to work. With UPS unable to ship a single package anywhere in the country or the world, FedEx's business doubled—a tremendous windfall financially but a strain on the company's workforce as well. On a typical night before the strike, FedEx processed about 2.8 million packages; during the strike, almost 4 million packages were streaming through its hubs. Employees worked around the clock to keep up with the increased demand, but some of FedEx's premium services, including guaranteed overnight deliveries, had to be suspended during those two weeks. Although FedEx customers weren't thrilled about the change and the delays it involved, most were just happy not to be waiting indefinitely

The UPS strike of 1997 involved 185,000 UPS workers and gave FedEx a huge boost in business for their packages, as some UPS clients were.

The strike weakened UPS's position as the country's leading ground delivery service and opened the door for FedEx to expand its own ground services, which hadn't been a major priority for the company up to that point. In 1998, FedEx acquired two companies—Caliber Systems Inc. and Viking Freight—that specialized in over-the-road deliveries to beef up its ability to compete with UPS. Because those acquisitions integrated new services into the company's offerings, FedEx created a parent company, FDX Corporation, that would include its overnight delivery services as well as its new ground services.

As FedEx continued to grow, thanks in part to the acquisition of Caribbean Transportation Services in 1999 to solidify its position in the rapidly expanding Latin American market, it became clear that the company needed to revisit its identity and unite all services under one recognizable brand. In 2000, the parent company FDX Corporation became known as FedEx Corporation. The core overnight shipping part of the business changed its name to FedEx Express, which was meant to differentiate it from FedEx Ground, the new name given to its over-the-road delivery service. The company also introduced new specialty services, including FedEx Global Logistics, which coordinated international services; FedEx Custom Critical, which included same-day and overnight delivery of "critical" freight, with special security features; and FedEx Services, which included a range of business and shipping services. Just a month later, it also announced the arrival of FedEx Trade Networks, which helped manage the necessary paperwork and legal issues associated with bringing products from another country into the U.S.

At the end of 2000, FedEx's revenues had grown to $18.3 billion, leading to a surge in profits as well. With new names, new logos, and new color schemes in place for all of its divisions, the company seemed ready to start the new millennium in style.

> "Complacency is a death sentence. When things are at their best, that is when you have to be most on your guard against complacency or getting in your comfort zone."
>
> FRED SMITH, FEDEX FOUNDER

FedEx Ground provided an economical means of shipping items that did not require urgent delivery

In the 2000 movie *Cast Away*, actor Tom Hanks plays a FedEx executive who is stranded on a remote island after his FedEx plane crashes in the middle of the Pacific Ocean. Hanks's character spends four years on the island, keeping an undelivered FedEx package safe all that time. When he launches himself back into the ocean on a homemade raft, he hauls the package with him, and when he is rescued and returns to Memphis, he is greeted by FedEx CEO Fred Smith—played by Fred Smith himself. In the final moments of the movie, Hanks's character delivers the package. Although FedEx's logo receives prominent placement throughout the film, the company didn't pay anything for the promotion of its product. FedEx executives loved everything about the movie—but the beginning, in which the FedEx plane crashes, gave executives "a heart attack at first," according to Gayle Christensen, the company's director of global brand management.

CHAPTER FIVE

Still Soaring

FedEx Express's presence throughout the U.S. became even more widespread in 2001, when the company forged a groundbreaking alliance with the U.S. Postal Service, which at one time had been considered a competitor. Now the two distinct entities were willing to work together to improve the services each could offer.

FedEx Express agreed to carry up to 3.3 million pounds (1.4 million kg) of U.S. mail on its airplanes daily, and the Postal Service allowed FedEx to place its drop boxes at post offices nationwide.

But because UPS was still a major competitor for ground business, FedEx made another acquisition to strengthen its own over-the-road services. In 2001, it purchased American Freightways and then combined it with Viking Freight into a new division given the name FedEx Freight. The new entity hauled larger, heavier shipments such as appliances and machinery over highways across the country.

The company further enhanced its ground business in 2003, when it introduced its first hybrid-electric trucks. The new trucks used a combination of electrical power and regular fuel and were designed to reduce smog-causing **emissions** by 75

FedEx's cooperation with the U.S. Postal Service in the early 2000s proved to be a fruitful partnership

percent. They marked the company's first step toward reducing fuel needs and improving the efficiency of its fleet. By the end of 2004, 18 of these hybrid trucks were making FedEx deliveries in cities such as New York, Houston, Washington, and Denver.

FedEx's commitment to becoming more environmentally friendly wasn't just about incorporating hybrids—and, eventually, some all-electric vehicles—into its fleet. It also experimented with trucks fueled by **biodiesel** in Washington, D.C., and with compressed natural gas vehicles, which produce 90 percent fewer emissions than gasoline, in Italy. In some of the largest cities it served, including New York and London, the company's couriers often delivered packages on foot or by bicycle. And in 2005, FedEx unveiled an enormous installation of solar panels at its hub in Oakland. The panels provided almost 80 percent of the power necessary to run the facility at its peak load.

As FedEx was making efforts to reduce its **carbon footprint** on the planet, it was also working to expand its brand recognition among retail customers. In 2004, it purchased Kinko's, an internationally known printing and office services shop, for $2.4 billion. Suddenly, FedEx had a new physical presence in more than 1,200 stores around the U.S., including more than 400 that were open 24 hours a day, 7 days a week. The acquisition created a one-stop shop, originally known as FedEx Kinko's, where customers could create, print, pack, and ship almost anything. In 2008, the stores were rebranded as FedEx Office.

In 2007, FedEx and its 280,000 employees worldwide marked the company's 35th anniversary by posting annual revenues of $35.2 billion. But the next year, fuel prices began to rise, and the U.S. economy started a downward spiral into a **recession**, which bit into FedEx's bottom line. Shipping companies such as FedEx were among the first businesses impacted by the recession, since people were purchasing fewer products that needed to be delivered. The company reported quarterly losses in both 2008 and 2009 and was forced to delay the planned purchase of several new jets as part of extreme cost-cutting measures.

FedEx Kinko's is now
FedEx Office

FedEx Office was another victory for the company, boasting nearly 2,000 locations worldwide by 2012.

"Record high fuel prices and the weak U.S. economy dampened volume growth and substantially affected our bottom line," Smith said. The company, he added, would have to cut expenses if it wanted to continue making money.

Although revenues continued to drop into 2010, Smith's strategy appeared to be helping the company recover its losses. Just as FedEx appeared to be turning the corner financially and heading into better times, however, it encountered more trouble: terrorists used the shipping company to send dangerous explosives overseas. In October 2010, bombs disguised as printer ink cartridges were found in a FedEx facility in Dubai, India, and on a UPS plane in England.

The threat of terrorism and the need for upgraded security measures weren't the only issues that FedEx would have to consider in the future. Smith, who had founded the company when he was just 27 years old, turned 66 in 2010 and admitted that he had begun pondering the possibility of retirement—perhaps within the next 5 years. "For the moment, I believe I'm in very good health. I play tennis all the time, I'm active, I enjoy what I'm doing," he said. "But obviously, I'm not going to do this forever."

In the meantime, he was planning on being part of his company's continued success. International growth, especially in Asia, remained a priority, as did the possible expansion of the hub in Indianapolis, Indiana. The company was also committed to becoming as green as possible by investigating the most **sustainable** options for all of its vehicles, from trucks and vans to airplanes.

Innovation was part of FedEx's founding back when Fred Smith wrote about his novel idea for an overnight delivery service as a college student. It's still part of the company's culture today. Throughout its history, FedEx has continuously looked for opportunities to improve its services and build a better business. That commitment to excellence has helped solidify its reputation as one of the foremost international shipping companies in the world.

"I believe we engineer time. I believe that as the world shrinks and changes, we offer solutions that allow you to engineer time to make things happen along time schedules that weren't possible."

ROB CARTER, FEDEX CHIEF INFORMATION OFFICER

Delivered by plane, truck, or foot, FedEx packages are today a vital part of countless businesses

FEDEX

SPECIAL DELIVERIES

Almost any package that FedEx delivers is special to the person receiving it. But among the millions of business documents, computer parts, and holiday gifts that FedEx has delivered to its customers worldwide are a handful of extra-special deliveries. The company once flew a two-year-old dolphin that had been rescued near Houston, Texas, to its new home at Six Flags Marine World. It renamed one of its jets "The FedEx PandaExpress" during a 15-hour flight that transported two giant pandas from China to the Memphis Zoo. It hauled 90 tons (80 t) of *Titanic* artifacts, including a 3,000-pound (1,360 kg) piece of the ship's hull, from Italy to Georgia, and carried the "Spirit of Liberty" Bell from Pennsylvania to Texas for the Veterans of Foreign Wars Foundation. FedEx has also shipped medicine, food, water, and clothing to such disaster zones as China's Sichuan Province, following a major earthquake in 2008.

GLOSSARY

acquisition the purchase of one company by another

acronym a word formed from the first letters of other words

allocation an amount or portion of a resource assigned to a particular recipient

bankruptcy the state of having no money or other valuable belongings, such as property, or being unable to repay debts

biodiesel a fuel that is derived from a plant source, such as soybean oil

brand the name of a product or manufacturer; a brand distinguishes a product from similar products made by other manufacturers

carbon footprint a measure of the amount of carbon dioxide produced by a person, a building, a business, or a product; too much carbon dioxide can have a negative impact on the environment

courier a person or company who delivers messages, mail, or packages

economics the study of how wealth and goods are produced, distributed, and consumed within a society

embargo a legal prohibition on the buying or selling of a particular product or of goods from a particular country or organization

emissions the waste created by the operation of an engine and released into the air

hangar a large, enclosed area for housing and repairing aircraft

incorporated formed a firm or company into a corporation by completing all of the required procedures and paperwork

infrastructure the underlying foundation and framework of an organization or company, which includes its employees and leaders as well as buildings and equipment

lobbying trying to influence the decisions and actions of public officials

profits the amount of money that a business keeps after subtracting expenses from income

recession a period of decline in the financial stability of a country or society that typically includes a drop in the stock market, an increase in unemployment, and a decline in home sales

revenue the money earned by a company; another word for income

shares the equal parts a company may be divided into; shareholders each hold a certain number of shares, or a percentage, of the company

stock shared ownership in a company by many people who buy shares, or portions, of stock, hoping the company will make a profit and the stock value will increase

strike a work stoppage that takes place to protest an employer's policies or to support a specific bargaining position

sustainable able to maintain an ecological balance by reducing the use and destruction of natural resources

union an organization of workers who join together to protect their common interest and to improve the conditions of their employment, including wages and hours

venture capital money invested in a new, high-risk company or organization that gives the investors an ownership stake in that organization

SELECTED BIBLIOGRAPHY

Birla, Madan. *FedEx Delivers: How the World's Leading Shipping Company Keeps Innovating and Outperforming the Competition*. Hoboken, N.J.: John Wiley & Sons, 2005.

Boyle, Matthew. "Why FedEx is Flying High." *CNN Money*, November 1, 2004. http://money.cnn.com/magazines/fortune/fortune_archive/2004/11/01/8189579/index.htm.

Cast Away. DVD. Directed by Robert Zemeckis. 2000. Los Angeles: Fox Home Entertainment, 2002.

FedEx. "FedEx Timeline." FedEx. http://about.fedex .designcdt.com/our_company/company_information/ fedex_history/fedex_timeline.

Foust, Dean. "Frederick W. Smith: No Overnight Success." *Bloomberg Businessweek*, September 20, 2004. http://www.businessweek.com/magazine/content/04_38/ b3900031_mz072.htm.

Frock, Roger. *Changing How the World Does Business*. San Francisco: Berrett-Koehler Publishers, 2006.

Wetherbe, James C. *The World on Time*. Santa Monica, Calif.: Knowledge Exchange, 1996.

INDEX